DATE DUE		

973.2
SAN

Santella, Andrew.

The French and
Indian War

The French and Indian War

by Andrew Santella

Content Adviser: Julie Richter, Ph.D.,
Independent Scholar and Consultant,
Colonial Williamsburg Foundation

Reading Adviser: Dr. Linda D. Labbo,
Department of Reading Education, College of Education,
The University of Georgia

COMPASS POINT BOOKS
MINNEAPOLIS, MINNESOTA

Compass Point Books
3109 West 50th Street, #115
Minneapolis, MN 55410

Visit Compass Point Books on the Internet at *www.compasspointbooks.com*
or e-mail your request to *custserv@compasspointbooks.com*

On the cover: Benjamin West's 1770 painting, "The Death of General Wolfe"

Photographs ©: Hulton/Archive by Getty Images, cover, 5, 7, 9, 10, 16, 17, 20, 26; PhotoDisc, 4;
North Wind Picture Archives, 6, 12, 21, 27, 34; David Muench/Corbis, 11; Bettmann/Corbis, 13,
35; National Portrait Gallery, Smithsonian Institution/Art Resource, N.Y., 15; Stock Montage, 19,
29, 38; Archivo Iconografico, S.A./Corbis, 22; Lombard Antiquarian Maps & Prints, 24, 30;
Wolfgang Kaehler/Corbis, 25; canadianheritage.com #20264/National Archives of Canada C2645,
28; canadianheritage.com #10154/National Archives of Canada C-1086, 33; Time Life Pictures/
Getty Images, 37; canadianheritage.com #23005/National Archives of Canada C-140172, 39;
DVIC/NARA, 41.

Editor: Catherine Neitge
Photo Researcher: Svetlana Zhurkina
Designer/Page Production: Bradfordesign, Inc./Biner Design
Cartographer: XNR Productions, Inc.

Library of Congress Cataloging-in-Publication Data
Santella, Andrew.
  The French and Indian War / by Andrew Santella.
    p. cm. — (We the people)
  Includes bibliographical references and index.
Contents: At the forks of the Ohio—Setting the stage—The first shots—Disaster for the British—
Pitt takes over—Invading Canada — The war's impact.
  ISBN 0-7565-0613-1
  1. United States—History—French and Indian War, 1755-1763—Juvenile literature. [1. United
States—History—French and Indian War, 1755-1763.] I. Title. II. Series: We the people (Compass
Point Books)
  E199.S23 2004
  973.2'6—dc22   2003014440

TABLE OF CONTENTS

NOTE: *In this book, words that are defined in the glossary are in* **bold** *the first time they appear in the text.*

AT THE FORKS OF THE OHIO

It was a race. Both Great Britain and France hoped to build a fort on the banks of the Ohio River. In fact, they both wanted to build at the same spot. It was a place called the Forks of the Ohio, at the site of present-day Pittsburgh, Pennsylvania. It is where the Allegheny, Monongahela, and Ohio rivers meet. Whichever nation's forces got there first could control the area.

4

Modern-day Pittsburgh stands at the Forks of the Ohio.

In 1754, Robert Dinwiddie, the British governor of Virginia, sent about 150 soldiers to build a road to the Forks of the Ohio. Their commander was a 21-year-old lieutenant colonel named George Washington. As Washington's troops slowly cut their way through thick forests, they received important news. Native American allies told

George Washington

Washington that a French force was camped not far from the Forks of the Ohio. Tanaghrisson, who was a leader of the Seneca nation, told Washington that the French could easily be surprised. On May 28, Washington attacked the

5

Washington's attack on the French was the first battle of the war.

French. In the short battle that followed, the French commander and 12 of his men were killed. Most of the survivors became Washington's prisoners.

The race to control the Forks of the Ohio had turned into a war.

SETTING THE STAGE

Why were both Great Britain and France so eager to build a fort at the Forks of the Ohio?

The Ohio River was an important part of both nations' plans for North America.

Since the 1500s, the powerful nations of Europe had explored and settled parts of North America. France,

English explorer Henry Hudson sailed up the river that now bears his name in 1609.

7

England, Portugal, Sweden, Italy, Spain, and the Netherlands all sent ships across the Atlantic Ocean. Their fishing ships collected huge amounts of cod and other fish from North American waters. Trappers and traders gathered valuable animal furs from North American forests. Europeans built towns and trading posts on land where Native Americans had lived for hundreds of years. Each country wanted to control the natural wealth of what Europeans called the New World.

By the 1700s, France and Great Britain had become the main rivals for control of North America. The two nations had very different plans for their territory in the New World. France sent explorers, traders, and missionaries deep into the forests of North America to live alongside Native Americans. The explorers and traders built forts and trading posts near major rivers. They formed **alliances** with Native Americans who lived around the forts. They traded with Native Americans for valuable animal furs, then sent the furs to Europe to be sold. French missionaries

8

A French Catholic priest baptizes a Native American child in the 17th century.

hoped to convert native peoples to the Catholic faith. By the early 1700s, French territory stretched from Canada, across the Great Lakes, and down the Mississippi River to New Orleans.

Meanwhile, the British were building colonies along the Atlantic coast. British settlers came to North America seeking religious freedom, hoping to own land, or to get rich. Most of these colonists made their living by farming, fishing, or trading. They built more small towns and cities than the French. In fact, by the mid-1700s the population of Britain's

9

English settlers in Virginia build homes in the early 17th century.

American colonies was 20 times as large as the population of New France, the area occupied by French forts and trading posts. With their numbers growing, American colonists moved west in search of new land to settle. This often brought them into conflict with Native Americans, who wanted to protect their land.

For different reasons, both France and Great Britain wanted to control the area around the Ohio River. Rivers such as the Ohio were important because they were natural highways. The dense forests and rugged mountains of North America made overland travel slow and difficult. The quickest and easiest way to travel long distances was by river. France wanted to use the Ohio River as a highway for trade goods. British colonists wanted the land in the Ohio River valley for future settlements. They also wanted to keep France from gaining more power and more territory. Two great empires were about to clash.

The French and the British wanted to control the Ohio River.

THE FIRST SHOTS

France and Britain had been fighting for years to control North America. Between 1689 and 1748, they fought a series of three wars. They were King William's War (1689–1697), Queen Anne's War (1702–1713), and King George's War (1744–1748). Neither country could completely defeat the other. So in 1749, the French

French soldiers of the 18th century

began building a chain of forts from the Great Lakes to the Ohio River. Colonists from Virginia tried to stop them. Washington's attack on the French forces near the Forks of the Ohio in 1754 turned out to be the first shots in a new war between the two countries.

12

After Washington's victory, other French soldiers in the area learned of the attack and quickly chased down Washington's troops. Washington's men rushed to defend themselves by building a crude **stockade** in a meadow not far from the Forks of the Ohio. They named it Fort Necessity.

George Washington and his men at Fort Necessity

The French surrounded the stockade and killed or wounded so many of Washington's men that he had to surrender. The French commander, Captain Louis Coulon de Villiers, allowed Washington and his troops to return to Virginia, but he warned them to stay out of the Ohio River valley.

In Britain's North American colonies, the outbreak of war had an immediate effect. Colonists feared attacks by French forces and their Native American allies. In the summer of 1754, seven of the 13 British colonies sent representatives to Albany, New York. Their purpose was to make plans to defend themselves against these possible attacks. Benjamin Franklin, from Pennsylvania, urged the colonies to unite under a president and council that would organize their defenses. Franklin's proposal became known as the Albany Plan of Union. However, the individual colonies were not ready to take such a step. Leaders in each colony knew that forming a union meant giving up some of their own

Benjamin Franklin wanted the British colonies to unite under a president and council.

power to a central authority. Franklin's plan was rejected by the colonies.

The representatives of the colonies did meet with leaders of the powerful Iroquois nations. The colonists hoped to make allies of the Native Americans. However, the Iroquois remained suspicious of the British, and they promised only to remain neutral. In contrast, the French were able to get the support of many of the Native American nations of Canada

An Iroquois warrior of the 18th century

and the Great Lakes region. For years, the French had worked as trading partners with these nations, gaining their trust and their loyalty. When the French and Indian War broke out, trading partners became military allies. French troops, French Canadian colonists, and their Native American allies fought together on one side against British troops, American colonists, and their Native American allies.

16

DISASTER FOR THE BRITISH

The first task for British and colonial forces was to move the French out of Fort Duquesne. This was their new fort at the Forks of the Ohio. In 1755, the British government sent General Edward Braddock to lead the attack. Washington was made one of Braddock's junior officers. Washington tried

General Edward Braddock marches his men toward Fort Duquesne.

17

to warn Braddock that the French and Native American allies were masters of frontier warfare. He told Braddock how they hid in the woods and launched attacks. This way, the enemy could not see them to fire back. Braddock soon found this out for himself.

Marching with about 2,000 British soldiers and colonial militiamen in the woods of present-day Pennsylvania, Braddock met a smaller French and Native American army. That army quickly surrounded the red-coated British and began firing on them from the woods. The British fought back as they had been trained. Trapped in the open, they stood shoulder to shoulder and fired. Grouped together, they made easy targets for the hidden French forces. After three hours of heavy losses, the British finally retreated. Braddock was wounded and later died. The fight came to be called the Battle of the Wilderness, or the Battle of Monongahela, named after a nearby river. It was a crushing defeat for the British.

18

General Braddock was wounded at the Battle of the Wilderness and later died.

19

The British soon suffered more losses. French General Louis Joseph, Marquis de Montcalm, launched an invasion of the British colonies. In 1756, the French captured Fort Oswego, on Lake Ontario in New York. The following year, Montcalm led an attack on Fort William Henry, on the shores of New York's Lake George. The

General Louis Joseph, Marquis de Montcalm

British and colonial defenders surrendered, and Montcalm allowed them to leave the fort and walk to the nearest British post. However, when the prisoners left Fort William Henry, Montcalm's Native American allies attacked them. More than 100 soldiers and colonists were killed. Hundreds more were taken prisoner.

News of the **massacre** frightened the frontier townspeople of New York and New England. British outposts fell to the French, one after the other. France's Native American allies attacked frontier settlements, killing and making prisoners of hundreds of colonists. The colonies remained disorganized and unable to mount a defense. It seemed nothing could stop the French and Native American attacks.

Native Americans attacked British prisoners at Fort William Henry

PITT TAKES OVER

From its beginnings in the forests of North America, the war between Great Britain and France soon spread around the world. Both the British and the French received support from European nations. The German states of Prussia and Hanover sided with Great Britain. France's allies included

The French defeated the British at the Battle of Hastenbeck in Germany in 1757.

22

Austria, Spain, and Russia. By 1756, fighting spread to Europe, India, the West Indies, and other parts of the world. In Europe, this war was not known as the French and Indian War. It came to be called the Seven Years' War.

After its string of losses in North America, Great Britain was ready for new leadership. In 1757, William Pitt became **prime minister** of Great Britain. He began forming a new plan to defeat the French. He sent more British troops to North America to fight. Pitt used British sea power to keep French supplies and troops from reaching Canada. Most of all, the prime minister realized that the British would need more help from American colonists. British generals tended to look down upon the colonial **militias**. However, Pitt worked to improve relations between the regular army and colonists.

The first target in Pitt's plan of attack was the French fortress at Louisbourg, on Cape Breton Island off the coast of Canada. Louisbourg was an impressive stone fort that guarded the entrance to the Gulf of St. Lawrence and the

23

William Pitt (seated) met with General James Wolfe.

St. Lawrence River. It was called the Key to Canada. If the British could take Louisbourg, they could follow the river into the heart of French Canada. The British had tried to launch attacks on Louisbourg earlier in the war, but they weren't organized very well. In 1758, Pitt sent more ships and more troops to take the fortress. The British and colonial forces had more than 14,000 troops at Louisbourg—more than twice as many as the French defenders. The British were led by General Jeffrey Amherst and General James Wolfe.

British warships kept Louisbourg under constant fire. They also prevented supplies and reinforcements from reaching Louisbourg. After six weeks of fighting,

A cannon at the restored fortress at Louisbourg on Cape Breton Island

The French and British fleets clash during the attack of Louisbourg.

the fortress was badly damaged and most of the buildings
burned. The French defenders surrendered. About 8,000
French Canadian residents of Louisbourg were forced to
leave their homes and return to France.

While the British were taking Louisbourg, they suf-
fered another setback in New York. A British force under
General James Abercromby launched an attack on the
French force at Fort Carillon (renamed Ticonderoga) on

Lake Champlain in northern New York. Abercromby's army was much larger, but the general managed his attack poorly. The French formed defensive lines behind a barrier of sharpened logs set in the ground. The barrier, called an abatis, slowed the British attack. Under heavy fire from the French defenders, the British made little progress. Abercromby sent wave after wave of attackers into the abatis, only to suffer more and more casualties. Finally, the British retreated. Nearly 2,000 British soldiers were killed or wounded. The French lost fewer than 400.

The British suffered heavy losses during the attack of Fort Carillon.

The British capture of Fort Frontenac was a blow to the French cause.

Despite the French victory at Fort Carillon, the war was beginning to turn in Britain's favor. The British captured Fort Frontenac on Lake Ontario in August 1758. The loss of Fort Frontenac made it difficult for the French to send supplies from Canada to forts in the Ohio River region.

That fall, the French abandoned Fort Duquesne, and the British finally took control of the Forks of the Ohio. The British renamed the post there Pittsburgh, in honor of William Pitt. It was a fitting tribute, for it was Pitt's leadership that had changed the course of the war.

The string of British victories brought Native Americans over to the British side. The Iroquois nations had been neutral at the beginning of the war, but they took the British side once the British began winning battles. More than 1,000 Iroquois warriors joined British forces in New York. They helped the British capture Fort Niagara on Lake Ontario. Cut off from Canada by the loss of Fort Niagara, the French had to abandon several other forts on the Great Lakes, as well.

George Washington and his troops watch as the British flag is raised over Fort Duquesne.

29

INVADING CANADA

In 1759, the British began launching their long-awaited invasion of Canada. The first step was to make another attack on the French at Fort Carillon. This time, as the British approached, the French retreated and blew up their guns and **ammunition** to keep them from falling into British hands. Led by General Jeffrey Amherst, the British captured the fort and renamed it Fort Ticonderoga. The British now controlled Lake Champlain. Another path into Canada was clear.

British generals who fought in the French and Indian War

In the summer of that year, a British fleet began heading up the St. Lawrence River. It included more than

200 ships and about 9,000 troops under the command of James Wolfe. Its target was Quebec. Taking Quebec would be no easy task. The city sat atop high **bluffs** overlooking the St. Lawrence River and was surrounded by a strong wall. Defending it were troops led by the Marquis de Montcalm.

Wolfe set up camp across the river from Quebec and began looking for a way to attack the city. There seemed to

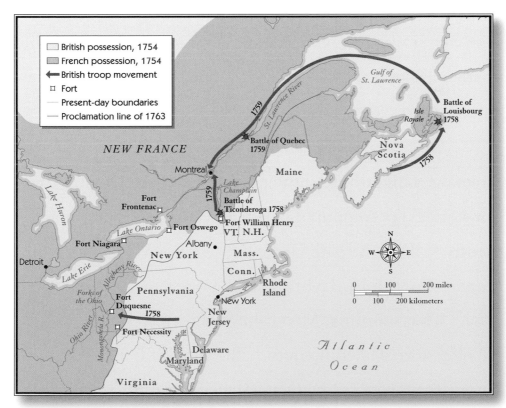

Troop movements and battles

be no way to send troops up Quebec's steep bluffs. For three months, Wolfe looked for a gap in the French defenses. He made a few attacks, only to be pushed back with heavy losses. By September, he was growing concerned about the fierce Canadian winter that was not far off. He would have to act quickly. Then, he found the opportunity he was looking for. A former British prisoner told Wolfe about a narrow path that led from the river up the bluffs toward the city. It was just wide enough for a few soldiers, but the path was not heavily defended. Wolfe decided to launch an attack there.

On September 13, he sent 1,700 troops across the river to make a nighttime landing below the cliffs. Quietly, the first attackers crept up the path and surprised the French sentries. With the path cleared, the rest of Wolfe's attacking force followed. By daybreak, they were atop the bluffs.

That morning, Montcalm was surprised to see Wolfe's forces lined up outside the gates of Quebec. What's more, they were ready to attack where the city's defenses

General Wolfe makes his way to the top of the cliffs near Quebec.

were weakest. The British formed their lines on a level stretch of land called the Plains of Abraham. Montcalm gathered his troops and decided to attack before the British could organize themselves.

A Frederic Remington drawing of the Battle of the Plains of Abraham

With flags waving and drums beating, the French advanced toward the British line. The British held their fire until the French were within 60 yards (55 meters). Then, all at once, they fired into the French troops. Stunned by the intense fire, the French retreated. In the fighting that day, both Wolfe and Montcalm were killed. When the smoke cleared, the British had driven the French defenders from Quebec. What remained of the French forces retreated toward Montreal. On September 18, 1759, the British marched into Quebec.

34

General Montcalm died from wounds suffered in the battle for Quebec.

The battle for Quebec was France's last chance to hold on to power in North America. The war with Great Britain dragged on, but never again would the French be able to challenge British control. After conquering Quebec, the British won control of Montreal and then Detroit. One by one, French cities and forts fell to the British.

Fighting continued in Europe, Africa, India, and the West Indies. However, France and its allies were not doing any better there, either. By 1763, both France and Great Britain were ready for peace.

THE WAR'S IMPACT

The immediate results of the war were spelled out in the 1763 treaty known as the Peace of Paris. France agreed to give up all of Canada, as well as its claims to India. France's Spanish allies also gave up the Florida territory. The British now controlled all of North America east of the Mississippi River. France's empire in North America was crushed. Great Britain stood as the world's greatest colonial power.

The war had other results that would continue to be felt for years to come. Victory over France gave Great Britain more territory and more possessions around the world. However, Britain now had the difficult task of having to control these vast possessions. Defending its new territory would require thousands of soldiers. Before long, Great Britain sent 10,000 new troops to America to defend its colonies. The costs of such a large army were too much for the British government. So it

American unhappiness with British taxes led to the Boston Tea Party in 1773.

imposed new taxes on colonists. The American colonists protested that the taxes were unfair and became more and more unhappy with British rule.

Chief Pontiac urged Native Americans to fight British expansion

Native Americans continued to feel the war's impact, as well. Some had sided with Great Britain, and others with France, but all suffered in the years after the war. With French troops gone, settlers felt free to move west into the Ohio River country. They settled around British forts and began farming and hunting. In doing so, they made it difficult for the area's Native Americans to hunt, trade, and carry on their way of life.

The British government hoped to prevent fighting between colonists and Native Americans. It also wished to avoid the cost of defense in case a war broke out. So the government declared the vast land between the Appalachian

The Proclamation of 1763 banned settlers from moving west of the Appalachian Mountains.

Mountains and the Mississippi River a Native American reserve. Known as the Proclamation of 1763, the new law also prohibited settlers from moving west of the Appalachian Mountains.

The proclamation angered many colonists, who believed that the British government had no right to tell them where they could live. Many ignored the Proclamation of 1763. Settlers continued to move west. In the years ahead, many Native American nations were forced from their land or wiped out.

Angry about new taxes and the Proclamation of 1763, American colonists began to question British rule. They believed they had played a key part in Great Britain's victory over France in the French and Indian War. Now they wanted to enjoy the benefits of that victory. To many colonists, it seemed that the British wanted only to take away their rights. After the war, the relationship between Great Britain and the American colonies began to crumble.

The shots fired at the Battle of Lexington in 1775 were the first of the Revolution.

The colonists' complaints about British rule grew.
Their dissatisfaction would soon boil over in the
American Revolution.

41

GLOSSARY

alliances—agreements between nations or groups to assist each other in military operations

ammunition—bullets, powder and other material used in the firing of a weapon

bluffs—high, often rocky, cliffs

massacre—the killing of a large number of helpless people

militias—military force, often made up of local volunteers

prime minister—in many nations, the head of government

stockade—an enclosure made of posts or logs set upright in the ground

DID YOU KNOW?

- The Massachusetts town of Amherst and Amherst College were named for General Jeffrey Amherst.

- General Edward Braddock had four horses shot out from under him during the Battle of the Wilderness. He was wounded during the battle and died four days later. He is buried near Uniontown, Pennsylvania.

- James Fenimore Cooper's classic novel "The Last of the Mohicans" (1826) takes place during the French and Indian War.

IMPORTANT DATES

Timeline

1749	French claim Ohio River valley.
1754	George Washington's troops attack French forces near the Ohio River, starting war with France.
1755	British troops under General Braddock are defeated at the Battle of the Wilderness (Battle of Monongahela).
1756	French troops capture Fort Oswego; war between Great Britain and France formally declared.
1757	French troops capture Fort William Henry; William Pitt becomes prime minister of Great Britain.
1758	British and colonial forces take French fortress at Louisbourg.
1759	Quebec falls to British troops led by General Wolfe.
1760	French surrender Montreal to British.
1763	Peace of Paris signed; Proclamation of 1763 prohibits settlement west of Appalachian Mountains

IMPORTANT PEOPLE

JAMES ABERCROMBY (1706-1781)
British general in the French and Indian War; replaced as commander after failing to take Fort Carillon (Ticonderoga) from the French

JEFFREY AMHERST (1717-1797)
British general who replaced James Abercromby as supreme commander; successfully led the capture of Montreal

EDWARD BRADDOCK (1695-1755)
British general who led his troops to defeat at the Battle of the Wilderness; he died from wounds suffered in the battle

LOUIS JOSEPH, MARQUIS DE MONTCALM (1712-1759)
French general who successfully captured Fort Oswego and Fort William Henry, and withstood an attack at Fort Carillon (Ticonderoga); he died during the fall of Quebec

WILLIAM PITT (1708-1778)
Prime minister of Great Britain during the French and Indian War; Pittsburgh is named after him

GEORGE WASHINGTON (1732-1799)
Colonial soldier who led troops during the French and Indian War; he served as first president of the United States

JAMES WOLFE (1727-1759)
British soldier who led his troops to victory in the capture of Quebec, but who died during the battle

WANT TO KNOW MORE?

At the Library

Collier, Christopher, and James Lincoln Collier. *The French and Indian War: 1660-1763.* Tarrytown, N.Y.: Benchmark Books, 1998.

Maestro, Betsy, and Giulio Maestro (illustrator). *Struggle for a Continent: The French and Indian Wars 1689-1763.* New York: HarperCollins, 2000.

Smolinski, Diane. *Soldiers of the French and Indian War.* Chicago: Heinemann Library, 2002.

On the Web

For more information on the *French and Indian War,* use FactHound to track down Web sites related to this book.

1. Go to *www.compasspointbooks.com/facthound*

2. Type in this book ID: 0756506131

3. Click on the *Fetch It* button.

Your trusty FactHound will fetch the best Web sites for you!

Through the Mail

Fort Pitt Museum

101 Commonwealth Place

Point State Park

Pittsburgh, PA 15222

412/281-9284

To learn more about the French and Indian War

On the Road

Fort Necessity National Battlefield

One Washington Parkway

Farmington, PA 15437

724/329-5512

To visit the site of the opening battle of the French and Indian War

Fort Ticonderoga

Route 74

Ticonderoga, NY 12883

518/585-2821

info@fort-ticonderoga.org

To visit the stone fort that was the site of battles during the

French and Indian War

47

INDEX

About the Author

Andrew Santella writes for magazines and newspapers, including GQ and the New York Times Book Review. He is the author of a number of books for young readers. He lives outside Chicago with his wife and son.